Bibliographic information published by the German National Library:

The German National Library lists this publication in the National Bibliography; detailed bibliographic data are available on the Internet at http://dnb.dnb.de .

Imprint:

Copyright © 2011 GRIN Verlag
Print and binding: Books on Demand GmbH, Norderstedt Germany
ISBN: 9783656048985

This book at GRIN:

https://www.grin.com/document/180609

Jules Miller

E-Commerce Security Threats

GRIN Verlag

GRIN - Your knowledge has value

Since its foundation in 1998, GRIN has specialized in publishing academic texts by students, college teachers and other academics as e-book and printed book. The website www.grin.com is an ideal platform for presenting term papers, final papers, scientific essays, dissertations and specialist books.

Visit us on the internet:

http://www.grin.com/

http://www.facebook.com/grincom

http://www.twitter.com/grin_com

ESSAY

E-COMMERCE SECURITY THREATS

ATLANTIC INTERNATIONAL UNIVERSITY

October 20, 2011

E-COMMERCE SECURITY THREATS

Introduction

Electronic commerce is concerned with distributing, buying, selling, marketing and servicing products and service through electronic communication systems like Internet, extranets, e-books, e-mails, mobile phones, databases, and other computer systems. As the Internet security is a critical facet of e-commerce whereas consumers who shop online need to be reassured that their transactions are secure and their credit information is safe, the current essay intends to point out security threats of e-commerce.

Business to Consumers e-commerce (B2C e-commerce) involves at least four main points that can be threatened by a hacker. These are: the online consumer, the consumer's computer, the network connection between the consumer and the server of the merchant's Web site and the server of the merchant's Web site. Security threats are actually possible security attacks against B2C e-commerce system and can undermine its availability, integrity and confidentiality. Availability refers to authorized access to resources of an e-commerce system and integrity implies absence of modification of data while the latter flow from the sender to the receiver. Confidentiality implies that only authorized people involved in an e-commerce transaction can read protected information.

Security threats against the online consumer

The possible attacks from a hacker can aim at tricking an online consumer to make the latter believe that he/she is the merchant that consumer was looking for. To achieve his/her goal, a hacker can use social engineering techniques that imply surveillance of the online consumer's behavior and collecting information to use against that consumer.

In his article *"Social engineering: 3 examples of human hacking"*, posted on http://www.csoonline.com/article/663329/social-engineering-3-examples-of-human-hacking, accessed on July 25, 2011 at 7:00 p.m GMT, *Joan Goodchild* highlights the remarkable talents of a social engineering expert named Chris *Hadnagy* who was hired as a social engineering auditor to access the servers of a printing company that had many competitors. Even if in the beginning the Chief Executive Office of that company stated that hacking him would be hardly possible, *Hadnagy* managed to achieve his objective by using subtle tactics that can also be used by hackers against an online consumer.

First of all *Hadnagy* collected information so as to get to know where the servers were located, IP and e-mail addresses, mail servers, physical addresses, the names and job titles of employees, etc. He also got to know that CEO had a member of his family who had battled cancer and lived and that by that fact, he was committed in cancer fundraising and research. Via Facebook, he got other personal information about the CEO like his favorite restaurant and sports team. With all that information, he contacted the CEO by presenting himself as a fundraiser from a cancer charity organization the CEO had had relations with in the past. *Hadnagy* told him that they were planning a prize drawing to be exchanged for donations with the prizes including tickets to a game to be played by his beloved sports team as well as gift certificates to a great deal of restaurants including his favorite spot. Thus, *Hadnagy* proposed the CEO to send him a PDF with more details on the fund drive and the CEO agreed and even disclosed to *Hadnagy* which version of Adobe reader he was using just because *Hadnagy* told him that he wanted to make sure that he was sending him a PDF document that he could read. Soon after *Hadnagy* sent the PDF and the CEO opened it installing at the same time a shell that permitted *Hadnany* to access his machine. Thus, the PDF became like the Trojan Horse used by Greeks as a stratagem to enter finally the City of Troy.

Likewise, once a hacker has gotten basic information about a given online consumer, he/she can call that online consumer pretending to be a representative from a site visited (a merchant's website) and by that way he/she will get information that he/she will use to pose as the online consumer and to provide stolen personal information to the customer service representative at the merchant's website in order to ask the customer service to reset the password to a specific value. That will help him/her achieve his/her dishonest objectives.

Another way an online consumer can be attacked through social engineering is about phishing schemes whereby a hacker plays on the names of famous merchants' websites in order to collect authentication and information registration. For example, http://www.toshibadirect.com/td/b2c/home.to is registered by the hacker as http://www.tozhibadirect.com/td/b2c/home.to. The online consumer mistypes and enters the forged site and provides confidential information and the attacker will manage to send e-mails that will took as they came from the legitimate site. Thus, the link inside the e-mail will map to the forged site that will collect the needed information.

A hacker can also impersonate a legitimate merchant's website by sending e-mails to online consumers getting them think that those e-mails come from a legitimate online merchant asking them to go to a specific website (a rogue website) to update their account information.

Thus, in order to reassure online consumers, governments and online merchants would need to sensitize and to educate the online consumers about possible phishing schemes and other social engineering attacks.

Security threats against the consumer's computer

E-Commerce Security Threats

Possible attacks against the online consumer's computer are concerned with using tools like SATAN (Security Analysis Tool for Auditing Network) to gain entry into the online consumer's computer in order to carry out scans on a computer capable of detecting entry points into the consumer's computer. If the hacker finds opened ports, he/she can use various techniques to enter into the consumer's computer. Once he/she has gained access to consumer's computer, the hacker scans the consumer's file system so as to fetch personal information like passwords.

In order to reassure online consumers, governments and online merchants would need to sensitize and to educate the online consumers on the importance of installing effective firewalls on their computers.

Security threats against the Internet connection between consumer and the server of the merchant's Web site

That is about the security of Internet connection between consumer and the server of the Web site. There is a risk of interception of information sent over an Internet network. This is known as packet sniffing or network snooping. It refers to capturing packets going through a network. That means that if the server of an online merchant is not secure, credit card details of consumers and their other sensitive information such as usernames and passwords can be easily intercepted by other people.

Data flowing on a computer network like Internet can be seen by other machines. This is the case for example, for computers connected to a hub because all data flowing from a computer to another can be seen by other computers connected to the same hub. It is important to note that wireless access points that are not encrypted operate like hubs. That means that any wireless adapter that is within the range can intercept all the network traffic in the area. Thus, if an online consumer visits an open wireless hotspot, any one around in a library, a coffee shop, or on the street can sniff the data traffic.

There is the same risk with SMS banking whereby the default data format is in plaintext for SMS messages as the initial idea for SMS utilization was to send non-sensitive messages across the open Global System for Mobile Communications Network. There is no end-to-end encryption between the client and the bank server.

Thus, in order to reassure online consumers, an online merchant would need to use a server having a secure Internet connection with strong encryption, authentication, auditing methods and effective firewalls to ensure that sensitive information is not spied by hackers. Websites whose address starts with "https" instead of "http" are encrypted so as to secure their connection. Online merchants should use them. To achieve that, a Secure Socket Layer (SSL) is used. This is a protocol whose main task is to encrypt data between the

4

consumer's computer and the server of merchant's Website. When a merchant's Web page protected by Secure Socket Layer is requested, the internet browser is able to identify the server as a trusted component and starts a handshake to pass back and forth key information related to encryption. Thus, on a following requests to the merchant's sever, the information flowing between the consumer and the server of the merchant's Web site is encrypted in the way that the attacker snooping the network cannot read the contents of that information.

Figure 1: An example of a website (mail.google.com) whose connection is encrypted

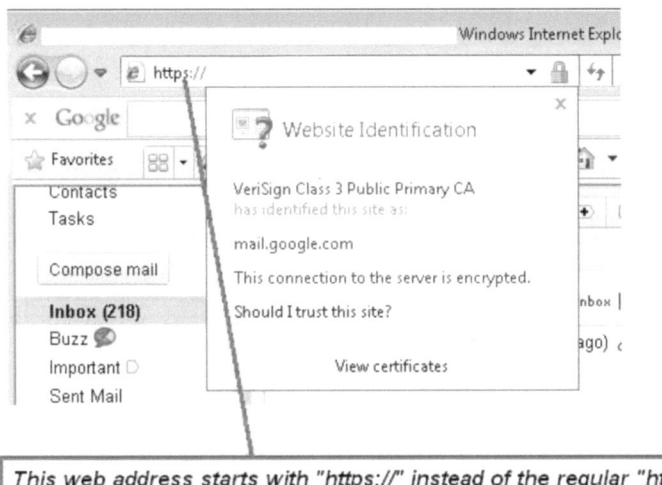

Therefore, in order to reassure online consumers, an online merchant would need a server using a secure Internet connection with strong encryption methods. The merchant should also choose a trusted online payment service provider whose system has proved to be secure and safe in terms of security of online payment transactions and safety of credit card information.

Security threats against the server of the merchant's Website

Possible attacks against the server of the merchant's Website can be performed using denial of service attacks, using known server bugs and server root exploits.

The denial of service attack implies getting the server of the merchant's Website to do a great deal of strange and useless tasks going beyond the capacity of the server to handle any other task. For example, computer pinging is used to build a DoS attack. Distributed DoS is such attacks whereby through a virus or another tool, a hacker infects computers on the Internet and those computers become slaves to the attacker. Then, the latter gains control over those computers at a planned time so as to bombard the server of the merchant's Website with a flood of mundane resource* consuming requests so as to cause the targeted server to experience problems. Such an attack will prevent legitimate online consumers from accessing information and service on the server of the merchant's Website.

As pointed out by *Mindi McDowell* on the Website of *United States Computer Emergency Readiness Team* (http://www.us-cert.gov/cas/tips/ST04-015.html accessed on July 26, 2011 at 10:45 pm GMT), in the article *"Understanding Denial of Service Attacks"*, there are no effective ways to prevent being victim of DoS attacks but there are some methods that can be used to reduce the risk of seeing the server become the slave of a hacker. Those methods include installing and maintaining antivirus software on the server, installing firewalls and restricting inflow and outflow of traffic to the server, and following good practices in regards with e-mail address distribution like applying e-mail filters so as manage unwanted e-mail traffic.

Another way of attacking the server of the merchant's Website is concerned with using known server bugs. The hacker studies the site to find out the types of software utilized on that website and to look for the patches (records of changes made to a software so as to fix bugs, add new features, etc.) that were released for the software. Then, the attacker looks for ways to exploit the server system without the patch and proceeds to try each of exploit. He can also find a weakness such as program bugs or any other weakness in a similar type of software and tries to use that to exploit the server of the merchant's Website.

Root exploits are other possible attacks against the server of the merchant's Website. Those are hacking techniques that allow to the attacker to gain control of the merchant's server and all consumers' information that is on the Website. To achieve that objective, a hacker can use buffer overflow attacks or scripts against the server. In buffer overflow attack, the attacker exploits a program bug that implies the allocation of storage during program execution and that involves tricking the merchant's server so as to make it execute code written by the hacker. For scripts, they are constructed by the hacker in the URL of his/her browser to retrieve information from the server, since knowledge of scripts to be

---

* The computer resources that can be affected are disk space, bandwidth, processor time, etc.

executed on the server can easily and freely gained through programming guides for the server.

But, even if that server was secured through modification of hypertext transfer protocol so as ensure encryption of data exchanged between it and web browsers and protected against external attacks, there would still be another security risk of theft of sensitive consumers' information by a person in bad faith who might have physical access to that server computer and use it for his/her own advantage. In addition, despite a secured server, the online merchant may not respect confidentiality of consumers' information and retransmit their financial information like credit card details on the open Internet without their knowledge and consent.

In order to reassure online consumers, server firewalls should be set up and strict software development processes including threat models by software vendors and external security audits are needed so as to reduce loopholes such as programs bugs that can be exploited by hackers. There also a need of setting up, display on the website and implement appropriate internal policies aiming at protecting consumers' personal information within the merchant's business organization.

Guessing passwords

Another possible attack against security of transaction and safety of credit card information of online consumers as well as the merchant's server is guessing password whereby the hacker guesses a user's password. For example, if an online consumer uses her husband's name or her National Identity Card number as the password, the probability of guessing a user identity and password increases as the number of tries by the hacker increases especially because there are tools that use words in the dictionary to test user identity and password combinations or that target popular user identity and password combinations. The hacker can even use automated password guessing to target many sites at one time.

In order to reassure online consumers, effective password policies including account lockout capabilities need to be enforced both for online consumers and internal users of the merchant's Website. The account lockout feature would also be useful because it ensures that an automated scheme cannot make more than a few guesses before the account is locked. Intrusion detection and audits of security logs can greatly help in preventing attacks and detecting potential hackers because they help understand the nature of the system's traffic. Thus, analysis of the security logs can detect patterns of suspicious behavior and such information will allow the administrator take appropriate action.

In addition to security logs, business auditing to monitor activities such as e-payment processing will help in monitoring and reviewing logs so as to detect patterns of inappropriate interaction at the level of the business process.

The following table summarizes the security threats against Business to Consumer e-Commerce and what can be done for prevention or defense.

Figure 2: Security threats and defenses

Target	The online consumer	The online consumer's computer	The Internet connection between consumer and the server of the merchant's Web site	The server of the merchant's Website
Security threat	-Social engineering techniques to trick the online shopper - Guessing passwords	Scanning the shopper's computer	Network snooping or packet sniffing	-Attacking the server through denial of service attacks, use of known server bugs and server root exploits -Guessing passwords
Defense against potential attacks	Education on how to prevent and cope with social engineering and on how to make strong passwords not easy to guess and how to protect them.	Installing and turning on personal firewalls on the consumer's computer	Strong encryption practices	-Installing and turning on strong firewalls and antivirus software -Use of mail filters - Using server software and the software running the Website that are strictly well developed -External security audit -Internal policies for consumer's and merchant's confidential information protection -Effective password policy analysis of security logs and business auditing

Conclusion

In order to reassure online consumers that their transactions are secure and their credit information is safe, governments, merchants, and computer system vendors need to promote the culture of security in e-commerce. Governments need to educate people on security issues and to give up-to-date information on the way of protecting themselves against attacks. Governments need also to set up e-commerce laws and to enforce them so as to take appropriate measures against cyber crime. Merchants need to purchase more sophisticated version of software applications that have strong encryption, firewalls and other security tools. They also need to set up within their business organizations policies regarding security of information systems and should include statements on privacy and security in their websites text and graphics so as to assure online consumers. Vendors of computer systems should acknowledge that they need to be part of the solution to e-commerce security problems. Thus, they need to develop new techniques and new products so as to cope with current and future hackers' attacks. Through such commitment, safety and privacy will be promoted in e-commerce.

References

http://pubs.cs.uct.ac.za/archive/00000347/01/Security_of_Mobile_Banking_pa
per.pdf , accessed on July 29, 2011 at 4:00 pm GMT

http://www.csoonline.com/article/663329/social-engineering-3-examples-of-
human-hacking, accessed on July 25, 2011 at 7:00 pm GMT

http://www.fraud.org/news.htm , accessed on July 25, 2011 at 8:00 pm GMT

http://www.ibm.com/developerworks/websphere/library/techarticles/0504_mc
kegney/0504_mckegney.html , accessed on July 23, 2011 at 6:00 pm GMT

http://www.us-cert.gov/cas/tips/ST04-015.html , accessed on July 26, 2011 at
10:45 pm GMT

https://www.infosecisland.com/blogview/3912-Network-Attack-Techniques--
Network-Sniffing.htmln , accessed on July 23, 2011 at 8:00 pm GMT

International Trade Center, *Secrets of Electronic Commerce: A Guide for Small
and Medium-Sized Exporters.* – 2 nd edition, Geneva: ITC, 2009.

YOUR KNOWLEDGE HAS VALUE

- We will publish your bachelor's and master's thesis, essays and papers

- Your own eBook and book -
  sold worldwide in all relevant shops

- Earn money with each sale

Upload your text at www.GRIN.com
and publish for free